Beyond Good Grades

A Growth Mindset Guide for Teens to Build Confidence, Think Independently, Resist AI Dependence, and Achieve Real Success

Patty R. Adams

Cantelune Press

2026

financial, medical, or professional advice. The content within this book has been derived from various sources. Please consult a licensed professional before attempting any techniques outlined in this book.

By reading this document, the reader agrees that under no circumstances is the author responsible for any losses, direct or indirect, that are incurred as a result of the use of the information contained within this document, including, but not limited to, errors, omissions, or inaccuracies.

Contents

Thank You for Reading!

I hope you found *Beyond Good Grades*

helpful and enjoyable!

Your feedback is invaluable to me and helps others discover this book.

If you could take a moment to leave a review, I'd greatly appreciate it. Scan the QR code below to leave your review:

Thank you!

Patty

Visit the Cantelune Press website for more compassionate books that meet you where you are!
https://cantelunepress.com/

Introduction

Every high achiever knows the feeling: sitting in class with a good GPA, a solid reputation, and a quiet voice in the back of your mind whispering, "What if I'm not actually that smart?"

It's the fear that shows up when homework gets genuinely difficult, when a teacher asks a question and the answer doesn't come instantly, or when everyone else seems to understand something that still feels confusing.

This fear doesn't mean you're lazy or you don't have ambition. You just care deeply about success, and you secretly doubt whether that success is built on real ability or just clever performance.

This book is a practical guide to building something real – not just impressive transcripts, but actual competence, resilience, and the kind of confidence that doesn't crumble under pressure. The goal is simple: to help readers become people they can trust, equipped with skills that last long after high school ends.

The concept at the heart of this book is growth mindset – not as a vague idea about "believing in yourself," but a concrete set of choices about how to deal with difficulty, mistakes, and the uncomfortable process of learning.

Growth mindset means understanding that intelligence develops through challenge, that struggle is evidence of the brain building new capacity, and that real confidence comes from accumulated proof of capability, not from maintaining a flawless image.

Progress isn't always linear; some things are genuinely hard, and external factors matter. But within the space of what you can control, the choices you make about learning, struggle, and skill-building shape who you will become far more than any single grade or test score.

Chapter 1

The Secret Fear Nobody Talks About

You've probably never said it out loud, but the thought has crossed your mind more than once: "What if everyone finds out I'm not as smart as they think I am?" It's the kind of fear that shows up when you're staring at a homework problem you don't understand, or when the teacher calls on you and your mind goes completely blank.

Fear isn't a sign that you're not smart. It's a sign that you've built your confidence on something fragile – on always looking like you have it together, on maintaining a perfect image, on never letting anyone see you struggle. And the problem with that kind of confidence is that it disappears the moment things get hard.

The truth is, when you care deeply about success – when you want good grades, when you want to get into a strong college, when you want people to respect your intelligence – the stakes feel incredibly high.

Every challenging assignment becomes a test of whether you're "actually smart." Every difficult concept you don't immediately understand feels like evidence that maybe you're not as capable as everyone thinks. And the natural response is to protect yourself: avoid the hard stuff, use shortcuts when you can, and whatever you do, don't let anyone see you confused or struggling.

But the more you protect your image, the less you build your actual capability. The more you avoid looking dumb, the fewer opportunities you give yourself to genuinely learn. And over time, that gap between how you appear and what you can do gets wider and wider, making the fear even stronger.

By the end of this chapter, you'll understand why your fear of looking dumb is so powerful, where it comes from, and most importantly, why it's keeping you from becoming the capable, genuinely confident person you want to be.

You'll start to see that the choice isn't between looking smart and being smart – it's between protecting your image now and building real strength for the long term.

And you get to choose which one matters more.

The Fear of Looking Dumb: Why Your Brain Protects Your Image Over Your Growth

Your brain has a job, and that job is to keep you safe. Not just physically safe from actual danger, but socially safe from anything that might damage your standing in the group.

And for most of human history, that made perfect sense. Being rejected from your community could mean the difference between survival and death. Your ancestors who cared deeply about what others thought of them were more likely to stay in the group, cooperate effectively, and pass on their genes.

The problem is that your brain hasn't updated its threat detection system for modern high school. It still treats social embarrassment like a survival crisis. When you're sitting in class and don't understand a concept everyone else seems to grasp, your brain doesn't register this as a learning opportunity. It registers it as a threat to your social status. The same neural circuits that would fire if you were facing physical danger activate when you imagine raising your hand and saying something that might sound stupid.

This is why the fear of looking dumb feels so visceral, so immediate, so impossible to ignore. It's your brain doing exactly what it evolved to do: protect your image within the social hierarchy. The challenge is that in protecting your image, your brain is actively working against your growth.

Research on social anxiety in adolescents reveals how this protection mechanism operates. When teens anticipate situations where they might be evaluated, their minds generate negative predictions like "I'll say something wrong" or "people will think I'm stupid." These thoughts activate deeper beliefs about needing to appear competent at all times. The fear becomes self-reinforcing: you avoid speaking up to prevent embarrassment, which means you never get evidence that your fears are exaggerated, which makes the fear stronger next time.

This dynamic intensifies during adolescence because of how the teenage brain develops. The socio-emotional systems that make you acutely aware of social evaluation mature earlier than the prefrontal regions responsible for rational perspective-taking and emotional regulation. Translation: you feel the embarrassment and social threat more intensely than you can reason your way through it. Your brain is essentially running on a hair trigger for anything that might make you look incompetent.

The cost of this protection system becomes clear in everyday academic situations. A student might intuitively know the answer to a test question but change it because it seems too simple, fearing that an obvious answer signals they missed something complex. Another might avoid asking for clarification in class, operating under pluralistic ignorance – the mistaken belief that they're the only one confused when actually, several classmates share the same question. Someone else might spend hours perfecting the introduction to an essay, paralyzed by the need to sound intelligent, rather than moving forward with imperfect but genuine thinking.

What makes this particularly insidious is that the protection feels rational in the moment. Your brain presents compelling evidence: "If you ask that question, people will judge you." "If you admit you don't understand, the teacher will think you weren't paying attention." "If you try something difficult and fail, everyone will see you're not as smart as they thought." These predictions feel like facts rather than fears.

But the cost of always protecting your image is that you never build genuine capability. Every time you choose to look smart over becoming smarter, you reinforce the belief that your worth depends on appearing flawless. You trade long-term competence for short-term comfort. You prioritize how you're perceived today over who you're becoming tomorrow.

The teens who develop real confidence aren't the ones who never feel this fear. They're the ones who've learned to recognize when their brain is protecting their image at the expense of their growth, and they choose growth anyway.

Perfectionism and Performance Pressure: When Good Grades Don't Equal Real Confidence

There's a specific type of anxiety that comes with being a high-achieving student, and it doesn't show up on report cards. It's the feeling of getting a 94% and immediately obsessing over the six points you lost. It's spending three hours perfecting an essay that only needed to be "good enough," then lying awake wondering if the teacher noticed the one awkward transition in paragraph four. It's the exhausting performance of always having it together, always being on top of things, always appearing effortlessly capable.

This is perfectionism, and it masquerades as excellence. But they're not the same thing.

Excellence is about doing your best work and improving over time. Perfectionism is about never being allowed to do anything less than flawless work, even when you're learning something for the first time. Excellence motivates you to grow. Perfectionism paralyzes you with the fear that any mistake will expose you as a fraud.

Research on adolescent perfectionism reveals three distinct types that affect teens differently. Self-oriented perfectionism involves setting impossibly high standards for yourself and engaging in harsh self-criticism when you fall short. Socially prescribed perfectionism stems from believing that others expect perfection from you – that your parents, teachers, or peers will only value you if you're flawless. Other-oriented perfectionism means holding everyone around you to unrealistic standards, which damages relationships and creates constant disappointment.

The most damaging form for teen confidence is socially prescribed perfectionism, which has increased significantly among young people over recent decades. When you believe that your worth in others' eyes depends entirely on perfect performance, every assignment becomes a referendum on your value as a person. A single B feels like catastrophic failure. A confused moment in class feels like public humiliation. The pressure becomes relentless because there's no room for the messy, imperfect process that actual learning requires.

Perfectionism doesn't lead to better performance. Studies examining academic achievement and perfectionism find that while conscientious striving correlates with success, perfectionism correlates with anxiety, procrastination, and decreased performance under pressure. Perfectionistic students often achieve less than their growth-minded peers because they avoid challenges where they might not immediately excel, stick to subjects they've already mastered, and spend excessive time on low-stakes tasks to maintain their flawless image.

The performance pressure that fuels perfectionism operates on a simple but destructive equation:

Your worth = Your last grade.

When you internalize this belief, good grades don't build confidence – they just temporarily relieve anxiety until the next evaluation. You're never secure because your sense of capability depends entirely on external validation that must be earned again and again. A 4.0 GPA becomes a prison rather than an achievement because any crack in that perfect record feels like your entire identity collapsing.

This explains why straight-A students can feel profoundly insecure. Their confidence isn't rooted in genuine competence – the knowledge that they can handle challenges, learn from mistakes, and improve over time. Instead, it's rooted in an unbroken streak of perfect performances. The moment something threatens that streak, the anxiety floods in because there's no foundation underneath. They've been so busy maintaining appearances that they never built actual resilience.

The alternative isn't lowering your standards or stopping caring about achievement. It's understanding that real confidence comes from evidence of your ability to handle difficulty, not evidence of your ability to avoid it. It comes from the accumulated proof that you can struggle with something hard, make mistakes, adjust, and eventually figure it out. That kind of confidence doesn't disappear when you get a bad grade because it's based on being capable of growth.

The teens who develop genuine confidence aren't the ones who never stumble. They're the ones who've learned that stumbling is part of getting stronger, and that their worth isn't determined by whether they're flawless, but by whether they keep learning.

Why Struggle Feels Threatening (And Why That's the Real Problem)

The moment a math problem looks unfamiliar, something shifts in your body. Heart rate up. Palms sweating. Mind blank or suddenly racing: *"I should know this"* or *"everyone else probably gets it."* This is your brain's threat detection system firing in response to academic challenge.

That's why it hits so hard. Your amygdala, the part of your brain that handles fear responses, stays hyperactive during this part of your life. Research from Weill Cornell Medical College shows that once your brain registers a threat, whether that's physical danger or an unfamiliar test problem, it becomes much harder to calm that response down than it will be when you're older. Your brain essentially gets stuck in threat mode. It's nothing more than biology.

The problem gets worse when you layer a fixed mindset on top of it. If you believe intelligence is something you either have or you don't, struggle stops feeling like a normal part of learning and starts feeling like proof you're not smart enough. The struggle itself becomes evidence of a permanent limit, which is a pretty terrifying thing to feel in the middle of class.

And the stakes feel real, because in a lot of ways they are. Your grades affect class rank, college options, how teachers see you, how peers see you. So when you hit something confusing, your brain starts processing a potential threat to your reputation and your future. That's a lot of weight for a simple book passage or math problem to carry.

When struggle feels that threatening, avoidance becomes the logical move. You procrastinate on hard assignments. You pick the easier class. You find a shortcut to get past the confusion without sitting in it. And it works, temporarily. The anxiety drops. But your brain never gets the practice it needs, and the next hard thing feels even more threatening than the last.

Social comparison makes all of this worse. When you're stuck on a problem and your classmate seems to breeze through it, your brain reads that gap as evidence that they have something you lack. It doesn't occur to you that they might be confused at home, that they have a tutor, or that they saw similar material before. You just see that they get it, you don't. And that feels like proof.

Discomfort is completely normal when you're learning something genuinely new. The issue is what you've been taught to do with that discomfort.

When you avoid hard things to escape that feeling, you never build evidence that you can handle them, which makes the next challenge feel even bigger. The confidence gap widens because you've been protecting yourself from the exact experiences that would build it.

The fear of looking dumb isn't a character flaw. It's a survival instinct that your brain hasn't updated for modern life. The same wiring that once protected your ancestors from social rejection now convinces you that struggling with a calculus problem is a threat to your identity. Understanding that helps you change what you do with it.

Everything in this chapter comes down to one thing: what it means to tie your worth to your performance. When your value as a person depends on always appearing smart, never being confused, and getting top grades, every challenge becomes a test of whether you're "actually smart" instead of a chance to become a functional, capable person on the other side of high school.

This is why a great GPA doesn't automatically mean real confidence. A 4.0 built on avoiding hard classes, using shortcuts when confused, and obsessing over every lost point is a fragile foundation. And the moment something genuinely difficult shows up, it cracks, because it was built on your ability to avoid difficulty.

When you understand these patterns, you start catching the moment your brain flips from "this is hard" to "I'm not good enough." You notice when you're dodging a question because you don't want to look confused while you try. That awareness gives you a choice.

The choice you have, then, is between protecting how you look today and building who you're becoming. Real confidence comes from changing what struggle means to you, from threat to signal, from proof of inadequacy to evidence of growth.

Chapter 2

Fixed Mindset vs Growth Mindset in Real Life

Most people think mindset is about being optimistic or believing in yourself, but instead, it's about what you do next when things get hard. It's about whether you see challenge as a threat to your identity or as information about what you need to work on. And more than anything, it's about understanding that your abilities right now are just a starting point.

The tricky part is that fixed mindset thoughts don't announce themselves. They don't show up with a warning label that says "Caution: This Belief Will Limit Your Potential." They sound reasonable, even protective, like you're just being realistic about your strengths and weaknesses.

But when you start paying attention, you'll notice them everywhere: in how you talk about school subjects, in how you react to feedback, in which opportunities you pursue and which ones you avoid before even trying.

The good news is that mindset isn't fixed. The way you think about your abilities right now isn't permanent, and recognizing your fixed mindset patterns is the first step toward changing them.

You don't have to believe you're capable of everything immediately. You just have to be willing to question the story you've been telling yourself about what you can and can't do.

What Fixed Mindset Sounds Like in Your Head: The Inner Voice That Keeps You Stuck

The fixed mindset voice whispers thoughts that feel like facts, interpretations that seem like observations, and conclusions that appear inevitable. But when you learn to recognize its specific patterns, you start to see how it operates – and more importantly, how it limits you.

- **"I'm just not good at this."**

This is maybe the most common fixed mindset phrase, and it sounds completely neutral. You're not being dramatic or self-pitying. You're just stating what seems obvious based on your current performance.

But notice what this phrase does: it transforms a temporary state – not being good at something right now – into a permanent identity. It closes the door on improvement before you've even thought about whether practice might change the outcome.

Research on mindset shows that people who believe abilities are fixed interpret difficulty as evidence of limitation rather than as a normal part of learning something new.

- **"They're just naturally talented."**

When you watch a classmate excel at something you're struggling with, this thought feels like you're simply acknowledging reality. But it's really protecting you from the discomfort of recognizing that their success might involve effort, practice, or strategies you haven't tried yet.

When you chalk their success up to natural talent, you're telling yourself a story where your struggle means something is fundamentally wrong with you, rather than that you're simply at a different point in the process. It feels like letting yourself off the hook, but it also takes away your power to change anything.

- **"This is too hard for me."**

Notice the finality in that. Not "this is hard right now" or "I need help with this." Just a flat declaration that you can't do it. When you frame it that way, the problem becomes a mismatch between the task and your abilities, rather than the normal friction of learning something new. And when difficulty feels like a verdict instead of information, giving up starts to feel like the only logical move.

- **"I'll never be as good as them."**

This one usually shows up when someone else's highlight reel makes your own progress feel inadequate. You see them ahead of you and assume the gap is permanent. What that thought leaves out is trajectory, effort, and the fact that you're comparing your beginning to someone else's middle. It keeps your eyes on the distance between you instead of on your own path.

- **"Why bother trying if I'm just going to fail?"**

This one sounds almost reasonable, like you're being pragmatic. Why put in effort on something that won't work out? But underneath it, the goal isn't to save your time. It's to protect you from finding out what your secret fear that you're not capable. And by not trying, you also shut out any chance of discovering that you could improve.

- **"Everyone else gets this except me."**

This phrase makes your struggle feel like a personal deficiency rather than a normal part of learning something new. It filters out all the evidence that other people are confused too, and focuses only on the story that you're uniquely behind. In reality, most people struggle with new material. They just don't advertise it.

How Growth Mindset Works in School, Sports, and Friendships: Real Scenarios, Real Choices

Growth mindset shows up in the specific moments when you decide how to interpret what just happened and what to do next. These decisions happen in classrooms, on playing fields, and in social situations, often within seconds, without conscious deliberation.

In School: When the Material Gets Hard

Think about what happens when a student encounters a challenging concept in class. The fixed mindset response sounds like: "I don't get this. Everyone else seems to understand. I'm just not good at this subject." This interpretation leads to specific behaviors – zoning out during instruction, avoiding homework problems that look difficult, or copying answers to maintain the appearance of competence without building understanding.

The growth mindset response to the same situation sounds different: "This is confusing right now. I need to figure out which part I'm missing." This interpretation leads to different behaviors – asking clarifying questions, attempting problems even when the path isn't clear, or seeking additional resources to fill knowledge gaps.

Research backs this up: students who see confusion as a normal part of learning stick with things longer and end up with a stronger grasp of the material than those who treat it as a warning sign.

The difference comes down to how you interpret difficulty. One student sees hard material as proof of their limitations. The other sees it as information about what to work on next. That single shift determines whether you engage with the challenge or walk away from it.

In Sports: When Performance Doesn't Match Effort

Sports make mindset easy to see because the results are right there in front of everyone. You miss the shot, drop the pass, lose the match even though you've been putting in the work.

The fixed mindset response is: "I practiced and still messed up. Maybe I just don't have what it takes." That thought leads to pulling back in practice, avoiding risky plays, or quietly giving up when progress feels too slow. If effort isn't producing immediate results, the fixed mindset treats that as a verdict on your ability.

The growth mindset response to the exact same moment is: "That didn't work. What went wrong, and what can I adjust?" That leads to breaking down the mistake, asking your coach for feedback, and deliberately working on the weak spots.

Research on athletic development shows that athletes who keep putting in effort after setbacks, treating performance as something that can be improved with specific adjustments, make greater gains over time than athletes with comparable talent who don't.

In Friendships: When Social Situations Feel Uncomfortable

Social dynamics trigger mindset responses just as powerfully as academics or athletics. When you feel excluded, experience conflict, or struggle to connect with people, your mindset shapes your next move.

A fixed mindset interpretation sounds like: "I'm just awkward. Other people are naturally good at this, and I'm not." This leads to social withdrawal, avoiding group situations, or staying within a narrow comfort zone of familiar interactions. The belief that social skills are fixed creates a self-fulfilling prophecy where limited practice prevents development.

A growth mindset interpretation of social discomfort sounds like: "That interaction didn't go well. What could I try differently next time?" This leads to experimenting, observing how others navigate similar situations, or practicing specific social skills like active listening or joining conversations. Research on social development indicates that teens who view social competence as learnable rather than innate show greater willingness to take interpersonal risks and develop stronger relationship skills over time.

The distinction matters because friendships, like academic subjects and athletic skills, improve through practice and reflection. People who recognize this develop social confidence through experience rather than waiting to feel naturally comfortable.

The Danger of Labeling Yourself: Why "I'm Just Not Good at That" Becomes Your Reality

When you say, "I'm just not good at math," you're doing something that works like a self-fulfilling prophecy. If you believe you're not a math person, you avoid challenging math problems, skip extra practice, and check out during instruction.

Research tracking students over several years found that those who applied fixed labels to their abilities showed lower engagement, less resilience when things got hard, and higher rates of depression than those who believed their abilities could grow. The labels they gave themselves early on predicted how willing they were to attempt difficult material years later, even when they were perfectly capable of succeeding with effort.

What makes this particularly tricky is that labeling yourself doesn't feel like a choice. If you've decided you're "not creative," that belief feels like an honest observation about reality. You notice other people generating ideas faster in a brainstorming session and take that as confirmation. So you stop volunteering ideas in group projects, stop trying creative hobbies, stop practicing the skills that would develop your creativity.

Every avoided opportunity reinforces what you already believe.

And the same trap exists with positive labels. Research shows that being told you're "smart" or "gifted" can create its own fixed mindset. When the praise is about your intelligence rather than your effort, you start treating that intelligence as a fixed trait that needs protecting. You avoid hard tasks that might crack the image. You get more defensive about feedback. A label that was meant to build you up ends up making you more fragile.

The alternative isn't pretending you're good at everything. If chemistry is hard right now, denying that doesn't help. The shift is in how you describe it. "I'm not good at chemistry" closes a door. "I haven't mastered this yet" keeps it open. One describes a permanent state. The other describes a point on a trajectory.

When you decide you're "not a math person" or "not creative" or "bad at public speaking," you're not just describing reality. You're making a long series of small decisions that prevent you from developing those abilities. The label becomes a filter for which opportunities you go after, which challenges you avoid, and ultimately who you become.

Your abilities right now are a starting point. The question isn't whether you're naturally talented at something. The question is whether you're willing to do the work to get better, and whether you can start catching the labels you've given yourself and questioning whether they're actually true.

Chapter 3

Performance vs Competence

You study hard, you get the grade, and then the information just vanishes like it was never there. Did you actually learn anything, or did you just perform well enough to get the result you needed?

There's a massive difference between performance and competence, and most high achievers have never been taught to tell them apart.

- Performance is what shows up on your transcript – the grades, the test scores, the GPA that colleges will see.
- Competence is what stays with you after the test is over – the actual understanding, the thinking skills, the ability to apply what you've learned in new situations.

Performance gets you through sophomore year. Competence gets you through life.

The tricky part is that you can have great performance with terrible competence. You can memorize formulas without understanding why they work. You can write essays that sound smart without developing your own ideas. You can use AI to polish your work until it looks brilliant without ever building the skills to create that quality yourself.

And for a while, this works. You get the grades. Teachers praise you. Your parents are proud. You look successful.

But underneath, something dangerous is happening. You're building a foundation made of shortcuts, memorization, and borrowed thinking. It feels solid until you hit something genuinely challenging – a concept that can't be memorized, a problem that requires actual reasoning, a situation where you need to think independently without a tool to lean on.

That's when the difference between looking smart and being capable becomes painfully obvious.

Grades matter, and it's dishonest to pretend they don't. But if every study decision is about "what will get me the best score" rather than "what will help me understand this," you're playing a short game that gets more dangerous the longer you play it.

You're training yourself to perform rather than to think, and that's a problem that doesn't show up on your report card until it's too late.

Right now, you're making choices every single day about whether you're building performance or competence.

- When you're studying for a test, are you trying to understand the material or just memorize enough to pass?
- When you're writing an essay, are you developing your thinking or just arranging words until they sound good?
- When you use AI, are you using it to strengthen your skills or replace them?

These aren't dramatic, life-changing decisions. They're small, quiet choices that feel insignificant in the moment but determine who you're becoming.

Grades vs Understanding: Why Your A Might Be Hiding What You Don't Know

Grades measure compliance, completion, and test-taking ability as much as they measure actual understanding. Research consistently shows that nearly 60% of middle and high school grades don't align with standardized test scores that measure course knowledge.

That means more than half the time, your grade isn't reflecting what you know – it's reflecting how well you played the game.

Think about how grades are calculated in most classes:

- Homework completion, which rewards finishing assignments whether you understood them or not.
- Group project work, where one person's understanding can carry the whole team's grade.
- Extra credit for bringing in supplies or attending events.
- Participation points for raising your hand, regardless of whether your answer was right.
- Test performance, which can be influenced by anxiety, lucky guessing, or how well you slept the night before.

All of this gets averaged together into a single letter that's supposed to represent your mastery of the material.

The tricky part is that a good grade can fool you into thinking you've got it down when you really don't. When you see an A on your transcript, your brain interprets that as "I know this subject." But if that A came from memorizing vocabulary the night before, copying homework answers to stay caught up, or letting AI polish your rough draft into something you couldn't have written yourself, you don't have the actual knowledge that the grade claims you have. You just figured out how to play the game well enough to get the points.

This becomes brutally obvious when you hit material that builds on previous knowledge. If you got an A in Algebra I by memorizing steps without really understanding why they work, Algebra II is going to be rough because now you have to apply those concepts, not just repeat them. Same thing with history essays. You can score well by using the right vocabulary and hitting the format your teacher wants, but when a college class asks you to come up with your own interpretation? That's a different skill entirely – and if you never built it, you'll feel it. The grade said you were ready. Your actual ability is a different story.

Studies on feedback and learning back this up: students who only receive grades on their work show minimal improvement over time, while students who receive detailed feedback without grades perform significantly better on subsequent tasks. The grade itself teaches you nothing. It's a label.

When you fixate on it, which most people do, you end up asking "what did I get?" instead of "what did I miss?" or "how should I be thinking about this differently?"

This one's especially sneaky for high achievers, because you've gotten so good at working the system that you don't even realize you're doing it. But if those grades came from shortcuts and memorization instead of actually learning the material, you're setting yourself up for a much harder time later – when the work requires real thinking that you never had to build.

Looking Smart vs Becoming Capable: The Performance Trap That Weakens Your Foundation

There's a specific kind of student in every high school who seems to have it all figured out. They always have the right answer ready when the teacher calls on them. Their essays sound polished and sophisticated. They project confidence in class discussions, speaking with authority on topics they didn't even know about yesterday.

They look smart, and everyone treats them accordingly. But nobody sees that many of these students have become experts at managing perception rather than building capability.

Looking smart is about image management.

- It's choosing the easy elective because you'll dominate the class and look brilliant compared to less motivated students.
- It's speaking up in discussions only when you're sure your comment will sound insightful.
- It's using sophisticated vocabulary in essays even when simpler words would communicate your ideas more clearly, because complex language creates an impression of depth.
- It's letting AI elevate your writing to a level you couldn't produce independently, then accepting praise for work that doesn't reflect your actual capability.

Becoming capable is an entirely different process.

- It's taking the challenging course even though you might struggle visibly in front of peers.
- It's asking questions that reveal what you don't understand, risking looking confused in the moment.
- It's writing in your own voice and gradually improving it through feedback and practice.
- It's using tools to support your thinking, not replace it, so that your skills develop over time.

The student who's focused on looking smart stays in their comfort zone, showing off what they already know so their image stays intact. The student who's focused on actually getting better pushes into territory where they look confused, make mistakes, and ask questions that might sound basic, but they're building real skills. Five years out, those two students are worlds apart in what they can actually do, even if their transcripts looked pretty much the same.

The foundation you're building right now will only help you later. If that foundation is made of performance and perception management, it will crack under pressure when you encounter truly demanding work that requires independent thinking. If it's made of genuine capability built through struggle and honest learning, it will support whatever you want to build on top of it.

The Hidden Cost of Always Chasing Results: What You Lose When You Only Care About the Score

The real problem starts when your grade becomes the only thing that matters, and when every decision about school runs through one question: "Will this help my GPA?" Because when that happens, you start making choices that look good on paper while slowly chipping away at the actual skills those grades are supposed to show.

And it messes with your head too. When your whole identity is wrapped up in your GPA, every single assignment feels like it's about more than just the work. A bad grade stops being feedback – it starts feeling like proof that you're not good enough.

That's a heavy way to live. School stops being a place where you're learning and growing, and turns into a constant test of whether you're worth something. Every grade feels like a verdict on you as a person – which means the stakes never actually go down.

What gets lost in this relentless pursuit of scores is everything that matters for your future capability.

- You lose resilience because you never develop experience recovering from setbacks – you've been too busy avoiding them.

- You lose intrinsic motivation because subjects become obstacles to overcome rather than topics to explore.

- You lose deep understanding because surface-level strategies that maximize grades don't build the conceptual knowledge that transfers to new situations.
- You lose authentic self-knowledge because when your worth depends entirely on performance, you can't afford honest self-assessment.
- Perhaps most significantly, you lose the ability to seek help when you need it.

High-achieving, perfectionist students often resist asking for support because they view it as admission of failure. The very students who seems the most successful might be suffering the most, isolated by this image they feel compelled to maintain.

The difference between healthy goal-pursuit and destructive results-chasing comes down to one question: Are you working to become more capable, or are you working to prove you're already capable?

The first builds competence through honest engagement with challenge. The second protects an image while actual skills stagnate.

The difference between performance and competence isn't abstract philosophy – it's the gap between who you appear to be and who you actually are. Every day, you're making choices that either close that gap or widen it.

When you memorize without understanding, polish without thinking, or optimize for grades without building skills, you're choosing performance. When you struggle with concepts until they click, ask questions that expose confusion, or use tools to support rather than replace your thinking, you're choosing competence.

There's no moment where you consciously decide, "Today I will sacrifice my long-term capability for a short-term result." Instead, it happens in the decision to look up the answer instead of wrestling with the problem for another ten minutes, the choice to let AI elevate your essay beyond your current writing ability, the habit of studying for the test rather than studying to understand the material.

These moments accumulate into patterns, and those patterns become who you are.

Performance and competence can look exactly the same on paper. Two students can both earn A's in the same class – one through genuine understanding that will serve them for years, the other through strategic shortcuts that will leave them unprepared for what comes next.

The grade doesn't reveal which path was taken. Only time does that, usually when it's much harder to fix.

This chapter isn't asking you to stop caring about grades. That would be unrealistic and dishonest. Grades matter for college admissions, scholarships, and opportunities.

But if grades are the *only* thing you care about – if every study decision gets filtered through "what will maximize my score" rather than "what will help me actually learn this" – you're building a house on sand. It looks solid until pressure tests it.

Right now, you're choosing between two different futures.

- One path leads to looking capable while quietly depending on shortcuts, tools, and performance strategies that become harder to maintain as the work gets more demanding.
- The other path leads to becoming genuinely capable through honest struggle, deep understanding, and skill development that makes you stronger over time.

The question this chapter leaves you with isn't whether you got good grades this semester. It's whether you're building competence that will matter five years from now, when nobody remembers your sophomore year GPA but you're still living with the thinking habits you developed. Performance gets you through the test. Competence gets you through everything that comes after.

Chapter 4

The AI Dilemma

You're not wrong for using AI tools. They exist. They're powerful. They're everywhere. You cannot, and should not, avoid them completely. That would be unrealistic and honestly kind of pointless advice for someone living in your world.

AI tools aren't going away, and pretending they don't exist won't prepare you for a future where they're even more integrated into everything.

But every time you use AI, you're making a choice about your own development. You're either strengthening your ability to think, write, solve problems, and create – or you're outsourcing those abilities to a tool that will always be there to do it for you.

And the tricky part? The second option feels better in the moment. It's faster. It's easier. It produces results that look good. But it leaves you with an illusion of competence that collapses the moment the tool isn't available.

Think about the last time you used AI for schoolwork. Did you use it to check your understanding after you'd already worked through the problem? Did you use it to brainstorm ideas that you then developed yourself? Or did you use it to generate something you couldn't have created on your own, copy it with minor edits, and move on?

Be honest, because seeing this distinction is the difference between building real skill and building a house of cards.

AI can be an incredible amplifier of human capability, but only if you have capability to amplify. Let's make sure you're building that foundation instead of accidentally skipping it.

When AI Helps vs When AI Weakens You: The Line Between Tool and Crutch

The difference between AI as a tool and AI as a crutch comes down to one question: are you using it to extend what you can already do, or to avoid doing what you can't? That distinction sounds simple, but in practice, it's easy to blur the line without realizing it.

When AI is working for you, it gets out of the way of your thinking instead of replacing it. Say you write a draft on your own, then use AI to check your grammar or punch up your word choices. The thinking was yours – the analysis, the structure, the ideas. AI just cleaned up how you expressed them. And you actually get better at writing because you can see what stronger choices look like and learn from them.

Take the AI away tomorrow, and you can still write a coherent essay because the core skill is yours.

Now let's say you read an essay prompt, immediately open ChatGPT, ask it to generate three body paragraphs, copy them with minor tweaks, and submit the work.

The thinking happened inside the AI. You coordinated the process but didn't develop the analytical skills, structure the argument, or wrestle with how to put complex ideas into words.

Take the AI away tomorrow, and you're facing a blank page with no idea how to begin, because the skill was never built.

Research from the University of Pennsylvania shows this pattern clearly. Students using AI tutoring tools initially scored dramatically higher on tests, with some improving by over 100% compared to peers.

But when those same students took closed-book assessments measuring identical skills without AI access, their scores collapsed. They hadn't learned the material. They had temporarily borrowed competence from the tool, and when the tool disappeared, so did their performance.

That's the core danger of AI as a crutch: it creates an illusion of understanding. You feel capable because you produced good work. Your grade might even reflect that. But the competence is rented. The moment you need to perform independently, on an in-class essay, a standardized test, or a college assignment where AI use is monitored, the gap between what you can produce with AI and what you can do alone becomes painfully obvious.

There's also a difference between AI that helps you get to the work and AI that does the work for you. Something that translates text, reads it aloud if you have a reading disability, or breaks a big problem into smaller pieces — that's a real support. It's removing something that was blocking you from engaging with the material in the first place. The learning still happens. You're still doing it.

Compare that to using AI to generate entire assignments or solve problem sets without understanding the steps. Those uses don't remove barriers to learning. They remove the learning itself. The obstacle wasn't preventing you from engaging with the material. The material was the obstacle, and AI let you skip it entirely.

You probably already know which side of the line you're on. When you use AI, you either feel the satisfaction of having worked through something challenging with support, or you feel vaguely uneasy about having produced something you couldn't recreate alone.

That feeling is your internal alarm system telling you whether you're building capability or faking it.

The "Did I Actually Learn This?" Test: How to Know If You're building Skills or Faking Them

So how do you know if you're learning something or just going through the motions? The answer requires more honesty than you may be comfortable with, but it's the only way to protect yourself from building a foundation made of borrowed competence.

Independent Recreation Test

Close the AI. Put away your notes. Wait a day or two, then try to solve a similar problem or explain the concept from scratch. If you can do it – maybe not perfectly, but competently – you learned it. If you stare at the blank page with no idea where to start, you didn't. You coordinated a result, but the skill never transferred to your brain.

Research on learning backs this up. When you practice pulling information out of your own head without any help, you remember it a lot better long-term than if you just reread your notes or leaned on outside support while studying.

The struggle to recall and reconstruct knowledge without assistance is what cements it into memory and builds genuine competence. When you can't recreate something independently, it means the cognitive work happened somewhere other than your brain – and cognitive work is where learning lives.

The Explanation Test

Try teaching the concept to someone else, or at minimum, explain it out loud to yourself as if you were teaching it.

- Can you break it down into clear steps?
- Can you answer "why" questions about the process?

- Can you identify where someone might get confused and address that confusion?

If you can, the understanding is real. If you find yourself reaching for the AI-generated explanation or your notes to remember what comes next, you're working from memorized fragments rather than integrated knowledge.

The Application Test

This one shows whether you actually learned something or just got through an assignment. Take whatever you were working on and try to use it somewhere new – a scenario you haven't seen before. In math, that means trying a problem with different numbers or a slightly different setup. In English, it means analyzing a passage you've never read using the same approach. In science, it means taking a principle and applying it to a new situation. Real learning transfers. If it only works on the exact thing you studied, you didn't really learn it – you just completed a task.

Genuine learning transfers. Fake learning collapses the moment the context changes.

The Confidence Test

Pay attention to the confidence test, but interpret it carefully. Real learning creates what researchers call self-efficacy – a grounded belief that you can handle similar challenges because you've successfully worked through the cognitive process before. This feels different from the artificial confidence that comes from producing a good result with AI's help.

Real confidence is calm and specific: "I know how to tackle this type of problem." Fake confidence is anxious and vague: "I got an A last time, so I hope I can do it again." If your confidence evaporates the moment you face the task alone, that's your signal that the competence was never yours.

These aren't tests you pass or fail. They're just ways to see clearly what's going on with your learning. The point isn't to be perfect. It's to be honest with yourself about when you're building something real versus when you're faking it. Because once you can see that difference, you can do something about it. Change how you're using AI, change how you're approaching your work, and start making choices that are setting you up instead of catching you off guard.

Using AI Responsibly: Practical Rules for Protecting Your Growth While Staying Competitive

Using AI responsibly comes down to having clear rules for yourself that protect your growth while keeping you competitive. These aren't restrictions for the sake of restrictions. They're guardrails that make sure every time you reach for AI, you're making a choice that builds your skills instead of slowly replacing them.

- **Rule one: Use AI after you've attempted the work yourself, not before.**

This one principle does more to separate real tool use from thinking replacement than anything else. When you struggle with a problem first, even if you don't get all the way there, your brain is doing work that builds understanding. It figures out what it knows, what it doesn't, and where the gaps are. Then when you use AI, you're filling in specific gaps or checking your thinking rather than skipping the thinking altogether.

And the research is pretty clear on this. When you try to work through something on your own before getting help, you remember it better and get better at applying it in new situations. Students who take a real shot at problems before turning to outside support end up with stronger problem-solving skills than students who reach for help the moment things get hard.

Rule two: If you can't recreate it independently within twenty-four hours, you didn't learn it.

This is your accountability check. After using AI to help with an essay, a problem set, or a project, wait a day and try to reproduce similar work without any assistance. Not the exact same assignment – that's just memorization – but something requiring the same skills. If you can do it, the learning transferred. If you can't, you coordinated a result but never built the competence. This test reveals the difference between borrowed performance and actual skill development.

- **Rule three: Use AI for feedback and verification, not generation.**

Ask AI to evaluate your draft, identify weaknesses in your argument, or check your problem-solving steps – but only after you've created something yourself. This mirrors how professional writers use editors or how engineers use simulation software: the human does the creative and analytical work, then uses tools to refine and improve it. Studies examining AI tutoring systems show that students who use AI for formative feedback – receiving guidance on their own work – demonstrate significantly better learning outcomes than students who use AI to generate initial responses they then modify.

- **Rule four: Set a dependency alarm.**

If you feel anxious or incapable when AI isn't available, that's your signal that you've crossed from tool use into over-reliance. Genuine competence feels calm. You might prefer having AI available because it makes work faster or easier, but you don't need it to function.

Dependency feels different. It's the panic that sets in when you have to write an in-class essay or solve a problem during a test without digital support. That anxiety reveals that your perceived capability exceeds your actual capability, and the gap is filled by the tool.

- **Rule five: Prioritize understanding over completion.**

When you're tempted to use AI to finish an assignment quickly, ask yourself whether completing this task matters more than developing the skill it's meant to build. Sometimes the honest answer is yes – you're overwhelmed, the deadline is real, and you need to get it done. But if that's happening regularly, you're optimizing for short-term performance at the expense of long-term competence.

Every time you use AI, you're casting a vote for the kind of thinker you're becoming. Use it to check work you've already done independently, and that's a vote for competence. Use it to generate work you couldn't have created yourself, and that's a vote for dependency. Those votes add up quietly over weeks and months, building either a foundation of genuine skill or something that looks solid until it's actually tested.

The people who will do well in the coming years won't be the ones who avoided AI entirely or the ones who used it for everything. They'll be the ones who used it strategically, who understood that the goal was never to finish assignments faster, but to become someone who can actually think, create, and solve problems when the tool isn't there. That's what's left when the test starts and the real challenges begin. Everything else is borrowed time.

Chapter 5

Why Struggle Is the Gym for Your Brain

When something feels hard, the instinct is to back away, find an easier path, or assume it's just not "your thing." The message you've absorbed from years of school and social media is that if you're good at something, it should feel relatively smooth. Struggle, confusion, and frustration seem like evidence that you're in the wrong place, trying something beyond your ability.

But discomfort during learning isn't a warning sign – it's a growth sign. When you lift weights at the gym, your muscles don't get stronger during the easy reps. They get stronger when you push into that burning, uncomfortable zone where the weight feels almost too heavy. The resistance is literally what builds the muscle. Your brain works the same way.

When you have a problem that makes you feel stuck, when you read a paragraph three times and still don't quite get it, when you sit with a question that doesn't have an obvious answer – that's when your brain is doing its most important work. Neuroscientists call this productive struggle, and it's the only way your brain builds new neural pathways. The confusion you feel isn't failure. It's construction.

The problem is that struggle has gotten a bad reputation. In a world where you can Google any answer in seconds, ask AI to explain any concept, or watch a tutorial that makes everything look simple, the experience of not knowing feels unnecessary. Why sit with confusion when you can eliminate it instantly? Why feel frustrated when relief is one click away?

Because every time you outsource the struggle, you outsource the growth. When you immediately look up the answer instead of wrestling with the problem, you get the solution, but your brain doesn't get stronger. You've borrowed someone else's thinking instead of building your own. It's like watching someone else do push-ups and expecting your arms to get stronger.

This chapter is about changing your relationship with difficulty. The goal isn't to make you love frustration or pretend that struggle feels great. It doesn't. It's uncomfortable, sometimes boring, often annoying.

But once you understand that discomfort is the price of admission for getting smarter, stronger, and more capable, you stop seeing it as a threat. You start seeing it as evidence that you're in exactly the right place.

The people who learn to stay in the discomfort – even for just a few minutes longer than they want to – are the ones who build real capability. Not because they're naturally tougher or more talented, but because they've learned to interpret the feeling of difficulty differently. They've trained themselves to recognize that the burn means growth.

Right now, your brain is probably wired to avoid hard things. That's normal. But by the end of this chapter, you'll have the tools to rewire that response and turn struggle into your competitive advantage.

What Happens When You Avoid Hard Things: The Shrinking Comfort Zone Effect

Every time you avoid a difficult task, something subtle but significant happens: your comfort zone shrinks. Research from neuroscientist Dr. Adam Gazzaley at UC San Francisco shows that people who consistently seek comfort and avoid demanding activities accelerate their brain's deterioration. The neural pathways that aren't challenged begin to weaken, and your brain's capacity to handle stress, uncertainty, and complex thinking diminishes over time.

Research on the Yerkes-Dodson Law shows that growth happens at moderate levels of stress. Too little challenge leads to stagnation. Too much leads to shutdown. When you consistently avoid difficulty, more and more tasks get pulled out of your growth zone and into your panic zone. Things that should feel manageable start triggering anxiety because your brain hasn't practiced handling them.

The biological side of this is real. Without regular challenge, your brain's production of dopamine and serotonin, the neurotransmitters that drive motivation and well-being, starts to decline. Unused neural pathways weaken through a process called synaptic pruning, where your brain eliminates connections it doesn't use.

And it goes beyond school. When you get into the habit of avoiding hard things, social situations that require you to put yourself out there start feeling riskier too. New experiences make you more anxious. You get less and less comfortable with uncertainty. What starts as dodging a tough calculus problem can slowly turn into a whole pattern of playing it safe that creeps into your friendships, your activities, and your willingness to try anything new.

This creates an avoidance loop. The short-term relief is training your nervous system to find challenge increasingly intolerable. Over time, that shapes how you see yourself. When you consistently choose comfort, you start to internalize a story: "I'm someone who can't handle difficult things." That belief becomes self-fulfilling. Your sense of what you're capable of shrinks right alongside your comfort zone.

The good news is that the opposite is equally true. When you push past your comfort zone and successfully navigate something hard, you build real evidence of your own capability. Each time you stay with discomfort just a little longer than you want to, you're retraining your nervous system to recognize that challenge is survivable.

Why Frustration Means Growth: Understanding the Feeling of Your Brain Building Capacity

When a student sits with a difficult problem and feels that uncomfortable tightness in their chest, something remarkable is happening inside their brain. That sensation – the frustration, the mental strain, the feeling that their brain is working harder than usual – isn't a sign that they've hit their limit. It's the feeling of their brain literally building new capacity.

The difference between students who keep growing and students who stagnate comes down to how they read that feeling. Studies on how students respond to frustration found that kids with a growth mindset pay more attention after they make a mistake, not less. They look at the feedback more carefully and do better on the next try. Their brains have learned to use the frustration as information about what to fix instead of just feeling bad about getting it wrong.

Students with fixed mindsets, by contrast, show heightened emotional distress and decreased attention to errors – they're so focused on the feeling of inadequacy that they miss the learning opportunity embedded in the struggle.

When you consistently take the easy way out, using AI to skip the thinking, looking up answers instead of trying first, avoiding anything that feels hard, you're not just missing out on learning the specific material. You're missing the chance to build your brain's ability to handle hard things at all.

The frustration isn't a bug in the learning process. It's the entire point. That uncomfortable feeling is what growth feels like from the inside. Students who learn to recognize it, tolerate it, and even expect it are the ones who transform struggle into capability. They've learned to read their own internal signals differently, understanding that the burn means their brain is building exactly what they need.

Rewiring Your Reaction to Difficulty: From Threat Response to Growth Signal

When something hard shows up, your brain makes a split-second call: is this a threat or an opportunity? That one assessment determines everything that follows. Whether you lean in or shut down. Whether you're thinking clearly or just trying to survive the moment.

Research on how students relate to stress shows that when you learn to see stress as something that's gearing you up rather than taking you down, something shifts in your brain. That racing heart that used to feel like panic starts feeling like your body getting ready. The mental strain that used to feel like you weren't smart enough starts feeling like your brain working hard. The way you interpret the feeling changes the feeling itself.

Research on stress mindsets demonstrates that when students learn to view stress as an enhancing force rather than a debilitating one, their brain chemistry shifts. The same elevated heart rate that felt like panic becomes recognized as preparation. The same mental strain that felt like inadequacy becomes understood as cognitive effort. The interpretation changes the experience at a biological level.

The rewiring process begins with awareness. The first step is simply noticing the reaction: that impulse to close the textbook, that urge to ask AI for the answer, that voice saying, "I can't do this." Recognizing the threat response as it happens creates a crucial gap between stimulus and reaction – a space where choice becomes possible.

The second step is changing how you interpret what you're feeling. When that familiar discomfort shows up during a hard problem, try shifting your thought to: "This feeling means my brain is working, not that I'm failing." That's not just positive thinking. It's actually accurate. Discomfort during learning really does mean your brain is actively building something.

Reminding yourself of that in the middle of a struggle, even when it's hard to believe, gradually retrains how your brain automatically reads difficulty.

The words you use matter more than you'd think too. Research on growth mindset found that adding one single word to a fixed mindset statement creates real changes in how students approach challenges. "I can't solve this" becomes "I can't solve this yet." That tiny addition shifts the feeling from "this is permanent proof I can't do it" to "I'm just not there yet." Over time, that habit actually reshapes how your brain processes hard things.

One of the most effective things you can do is start celebrating process over outcomes. When you train yourself to notice and value the effort you're putting in, the strategies you're trying, the adjustments you're making, you gradually shift what your brain finds rewarding. Instead of dopamine only coming from getting the right answer, it starts coming from engaging productively with the difficulty itself.

This doesn't happen overnight. Neural pathways that have spent years interpreting difficulty as a threat don't rewire quickly. But research on neuroplasticity confirms that consistent practice creates real, measurable changes in brain structure.

Each time you consciously choose to interpret discomfort as a growth signal rather than a threat, you're strengthening new neural connections and weakening old ones. Gradually, the threat response loses its grip. The growth response becomes the default.

The mechanism is straightforward, even if it takes practice. When difficulty shows up and you feel that automatic impulse to close the book, ask AI for the answer, or tell yourself you'll come back to it later, notice that impulse for what it is: a trained reaction, not an accurate read on your capability.

Then make a different choice. Stay with the discomfort for ninety seconds longer than you want to. Try one more approach before looking up the solution. Sit with the confusion instead of immediately eliminating it.

Those small decisions add up. Every time you choose to interpret struggle as a signal rather than a threat, you're reinforcing new neural pathways and letting the old ones weaken. What once felt impossible starts feeling difficult but doable. What felt difficult starts feeling manageable. Your brain adapts to what you ask of it.

The people who build this capacity aren't the ones who never feel frustrated or confused. They're the ones who've learned that frustration and confusion are temporary, and that they come right before understanding, not as proof that understanding isn't coming. The burn means growth. Discomfort is the price of becoming more capable. Real confidence comes from accumulating proof that you can handle hard things.

Chapter 6

The Comparison Trap

Social media has turned comparison into a constant background hum in your life, a never-ending stream of other people's wins, accomplishments, and seemingly effortless success.

The comparison trap is dangerous because it fundamentally distorts your perception of reality and redirects your energy away from the only thing that matters – your own growth. When you're constantly measuring yourself against everyone else's highlight reel, you lose sight of your own progress.

You stop asking "Am I better than I was last month?" and start asking "Am I better than them?" The first question leads to growth. The second leads to anxiety, shortcuts, and a fixed mindset disguised as ambition.

The truth is that what you see is almost never the full story. Social media shows you the outcome, never the process. It shows you the medal, not the months of training. It shows you the acceptance letter, not the dozens of failures that came before it.

The key is understanding why comparison is a rigged game you can never win. Someone will always be ahead of you in some area. Always. If you tie your confidence to being better than everyone else, you're building your self-worth on a foundation that can crumble with a single Instagram post.

Real confidence comes from tracking your own improvement, from having evidence that you're building skills and pushing past your previous limits. It comes from internal standards that can't be shaken by someone else's success.

When you learn how to build those standards, how to measure progress in ways that matter, you'll stop letting other people's highlight reels steal your focus from the only story that determines your future – your own.

Why Everyone Looks Ahead of You: The Illusion That Everyone Else Has It Figured Out

You're probably not going to believe this, but research on adolescent psychology shows that nearly everyone is experiencing some version of the same doubt, confusion, and struggle. The difference is that most people hide it well.

You're not seeing their internal experience. You're seeing their external presentation, the confident answer in class, the submitted essay, the polished performance, with all the anxiety, failed drafts, and self-doubt edited out.

Social media makes this worse by design. Platforms are built to showcase highlight moments and filter out everything messy and difficult. So you end up comparing your behind-the-scenes reality to everyone else's curated public image, and you always come up short in that comparison.

There's also something psychologists call pluralistic ignorance, which plays out in classrooms literally every day. A teacher asks if everyone understands. Most students are confused, but they look around, see others nodding, and nod too, assuming they're the only one who doesn't get it. In reality, a big chunk of the class is just as lost.

Everyone is performing confidence they don't feel, which reinforces everyone else's belief that they're uniquely behind.

The real cost of this illusion is that when you believe everyone else has figured something out that you haven't, you interpret your own struggle as a personal failure rather than a normal part of learning. You stop asking questions.

You don't seek help. You hide your confusion to avoid exposing what you assume is your unique incompetence. The exact behaviors that would help you grow are the ones you suppress to keep up appearances.

The students who seem most confident have almost always worked through the same confusion you're experiencing right now. Effortless success is almost always the result of effort you just didn't see.

Highlight Reels vs Real Work: What You Don't See Behind the Success Posts

The gap between what gets posted and what actually happens is huge. The student celebrating their debate team victory didn't post about the three competitions where they froze, or the nights they practiced arguments alone in their room. The classmate announcing their college acceptance didn't mention the two schools that rejected them, or the essay they rewrote twelve times. The athlete's championship photo doesn't include the early morning practices, the injuries, or the games where they played terribly and wondered if they even belonged on the team.

Selective sharing isn't dishonest, exactly. It's just human nature to share the wins and leave out the grind. But when you're on the receiving end, still developing your sense of what you're capable of, the effect is damaging. You see the outcome and assume it came easily. You assume the person posting has some natural advantage or secret knowledge you lack. The hidden effort disappears, replaced by the illusion of effortless excellence.

When you believe success should come easily because that's how it looks for everyone else, you start interpreting your own struggle as evidence that something is wrong with you. The confusion you feel learning something new, the frustration when progress is slow, the exhaustion after sustained effort, these are normal parts of growth. But they start to feel like personal failure because they don't match the frictionless image you're seeing online. That's where the fixed mindset creeps in: "If I have to work this hard, maybe I'm just not good at it."

Every success post is just the tip of the iceberg. The college acceptance came after months of research, drafting, and revision. The perfect test score came after hours of studying that nobody saw. The confident class presentation came after practice sessions full of stumbling and self-doubt. The work happened in private. The celebration happened in public. Social media shows you the second part and pretends the first part didn't exist.

Knowing that doesn't take anything away from what other people have accomplished. It just puts it in the right context. Success isn't effortless for anyone. It just looks that way when you only see the final moment. The real work happens in the unglamorous hours that never get posted. That's where the skills actually get built, one hard hour at a time.

Building Internal Standards: Measuring Progress Against Yourself, Not Everyone Else

The shift from measuring yourself against others to measuring yourself against your own past performance isn't a feel-good exercise. It's a fundamental change in how you build confidence.

- External comparison gives you a moving target that shifts based on what everyone else is doing.
- Internal standards give you a stable foundation: am I more capable than I was last month?

Research shows that people who focus on getting better at their own skills stay more motivated and stick with things longer than people focused on beating everyone else. When you measure progress against where you personally started, you stay in control of your growth. You can see improvement even when other people are also improving, and you can tell exactly where your effort is actually paying off.

It also changes how you handle setbacks. When a hard test gets measured against your own baseline instead of everyone else's score, it stops feeling like proof you're behind and starts feeling like information about what to work on next. Instead of "I'm worse at this than everyone else," the thought becomes "I need to change how I'm studying this." The keeps your focus on your own path.

The urge to compare yourself to others isn't going away. It's wired into us, and social media makes sure you're never far from an opportunity to do it. The goal is just to catch yourself when comparison is pulling your attention away from the only thing that actually matters: are you more capable today than you were before?

When your confidence depends on being better than your classmates, you're building it on something you can't control. Someone else's good grade or good post can knock it over. When your confidence comes from your own documented growth, nobody can touch it. It doesn't depend on anyone else having a bad day.

Comparing yourself to others creates anxiety. Comparing yourself to your past self creates growth. One keeps your eyes on everyone else's lane. The other keeps them on yours.

So, stop asking "Am I better than them?" Start asking "Am I better than I was before?"

Chapter 7

Perfectionism Is Not Excellence

Perfectionism feels like caring about quality, but it's about avoiding judgment. It feels like pushing yourself to be better, but it's about protecting yourself from criticism. And most dangerously, it feels productive when you're revising that introduction for the seventh time, but you're not building skill – you're just managing anxiety.

The difference between perfectionism and genuine excellence matters more than most high achievers realize.

- Excellence means setting high standards and working strategically to meet them, learning from mistakes along the way, and knowing when something is good enough to move forward.

- Perfectionism means setting impossible standards, avoiding anything you can't do flawlessly, and staying stuck because "good enough" never feels good enough.

Excellence pushes you toward growth. Perfectionism keeps you trapped in safety.

The students who achieve excellence – the ones who develop real competence that lasts beyond high school – aren't the ones who never make mistakes. They're the ones who make mistakes faster, learn from them, and keep moving forward.

- They turn in the imperfect draft and use the feedback.

- They attempt the challenging problem set even when they're not sure they'll get it right.

- They raise their hand in class knowing they might be wrong.

- They understand something that perfectionists don't: messy progress beats perfect planning every single time.

You can learn how to recognize perfectionism's warning signs in your own behavior, understand why the fear of mistakes is costing you more than mistakes ever could, and learn how to pursue excellence without letting perfectionism sabotage your growth.

The goal isn't to stop caring about quality. It's to start caring more about growth than about appearing flawless. Because the version of you that's willing to be imperfect while learning will always outgrow the version that plays it safe to protect an image.

Fear of Mistakes: Why Perfectionism Makes You Avoid the Work That Builds Real Skill

When you're afraid of making mistakes your threat response activates, flooding your system with the same chemicals as if you were facing actual physical danger.

Your amygdala – the part of your brain responsible for detecting threats – can't distinguish between the danger of a predator and the danger of looking stupid in front of your classmates. Both trigger the same fight-or-flight response, and for perfectionists, "flight" usually wins.

You avoid the challenging math problem, skip the advanced class, stay quiet during discussions, or procrastinate on the project until you can barely finish it, let alone do it well.

It makes sense that avoidance feels protective in the moment. When you close the textbook on a hard chapter or decide not to try out for the team, your anxiety drops right away. Your brain reads that as a win. Threat avoided, safety restored.

But every time you avoid something because you might not do it perfectly, you're training your brain that difficulty equals danger. You're reinforcing the neural pathways that say, "when things get hard, retreat." And you're systematically eliminating the exact experiences that would build your competence.

Building real skill requires challenges that push you just past what you can currently do, where making mistakes isn't just possible but guaranteed.

When you attempt something at the edge of your ability and make errors, your brain has to work harder to correct those errors, strengthening the neural connections involved in that skill.

This is how you develop expertise: through repeated cycles of attempting, failing, adjusting, and trying again. Perfectionists short-circuit this entire process by refusing to attempt anything where failure is possible.

What happens in a typical week when perfectionism drives your choices?

- You avoid asking questions in class because you're not certain your question is smart enough.
- You stick with subjects you're already good at rather than exploring new interests where you'd start as a beginner.
- You spend three hours perfecting an assignment that required one hour of actual learning, using the extra time to polish rather than to push into harder material.
- You turn down opportunities to present, lead, or try something new because you can't guarantee you'll be immediately good at it.

Each choice on its own feels reasonable, but collectively, they're building a smaller and smaller world.

The discomfort of making mistakes in front of other people fades. The cost of avoiding growth doesn't. And this isn't about being careless or turning in sloppy work. It's about knowing the difference between mistakes that happen because you didn't try and mistakes that happen because you're attempting something genuinely hard.

The first kind of mistake is avoidable and unhelpful. The second kind is unavoidable and essential. When you're working at the edge of your ability, it's a sign you're in exactly the right place for growth.

Every time you choose safe over challenging because you might not be perfect, you're choosing who you are right now over who you could become. The work that builds real skill is messy, uncertain, and imperfect. Perfectionism keeps you away from that work, and therefore away from the competence you want.

The Risk Avoidance Trap: How Playing It Safe Keeps You Stuck at Your Current Level

If you're a high achiever, you probably only go after things where you're pretty sure you'll succeed. You take the honors class in your strong subject but avoid the one where you'd struggle. You stick with the sport you've played for years rather than try the activity that genuinely interests you. You choose the group project role you already know how to do well instead of the one that would stretch you.

Each choice feels rational. Why risk failure when you can guarantee success? But collectively, those decisions create a ceiling on your growth that gets harder to break through over time.

Risk avoidance runs on a simple but destructive logic: if you never try anything where failure is possible, you never have to face failure. Your transcript stays clean, your reputation stays intact, your self-image stays protected.

The problem is that you also never develop new capabilities. The skills you have right now become the only skills you'll have later, because developing new ones requires attempting things you can't yet do well. Every time you choose the safe option, you're choosing to stay exactly who you are instead of becoming who you could be.

Think about what risk avoidance costs you.

- You might maintain a strong GPA by carefully selecting classes where you'll excel, but you're not building the intellectual range or the tolerance for challenge that college and careers actually require.
- You might produce polished assignments by sticking with familiar formats and topics, but you're not developing the creative thinking that comes from trying something new.
- You might participate confidently in discussions where you already know the material but go quiet when things get genuinely challenging, which means you're reinforcing what you already know rather than expanding it.

The people who make the most significant progress are the ones who deliberately choose challenges slightly beyond their current level and work through the discomfort.

- They take the class that interests them even if it's not their natural strength.
- They go for the leadership role even though they've never led before.
- They ask the question they're not sure is right, because learning matters more than looking smart.

Temporary discomfort is the price of long-term capability, and they've accepted that trade. The capabilities you'll need five years from now won't come from repeating what you already know how to do. They'll come from attempting hard things, adjusting when you fail, and building skills through messy, imperfect practice.

Every risk you avoid to protect your current image is a capability you'll never develop.

Why Messy Progress Beats Safe Stagnation: The Power of Imperfect Action Over Perfect Planning

Planning feels productive when you're really just procrastinating. You tell yourself you're being strategic and thorough when you spend two hours organizing your study schedule instead of studying, or outline your essay for forty-five minutes instead of writing the first paragraph.

Planning gives you the sensation of progress without the risk of doing something imperfectly. But research on skill development consistently shows that you learn more from fifteen minutes of imperfect practice than from two hours of perfect planning.

The reason comes down to how your brain builds competence. When you try something, even badly, your brain gets immediate feedback about what works and what doesn't.

You discover which concepts you actually understand versus which ones you only thought you understood. You run into problems you never would have anticipated in the planning phase. You build the neural pathways that come only from doing, not from thinking about doing. Every imperfect attempt gives your brain information it can use to adjust and improve.

Planning keeps everything theoretical. The plan feels safe because it exists in a world where everything works perfectly. The action feels risky because it exists in reality, where things are messy and uncertain.

This doesn't mean planning is useless or that you should approach everything chaotically. Basic planning, understanding the assignment, gathering what you need, blocking out time, is essential. But there's a real difference between planning that gets you started and planning that replaces actually starting.

Useful planning takes fifteen or twenty minutes. Excessive planning takes hours, feels like work, and keeps you comfortable in the preparation zone rather than in the uncomfortable zone where actual learning happens.

- The people who develop real competence start working on the problem before they feel completely ready.
- They write the messy first draft knowing they'll revise it.
- They do practice problems even when they're not sure how to do them.
- They ask the question in class before they've perfectly formulated it.

Each imperfect action moves them forward, builds their skills, and reveals what they need to work on, information that no amount of planning could provide.

Messy progress feels uncomfortable because it means producing work that isn't immediately good, making mistakes that others might see, and confronting what you don't yet know. Safe stagnation feels comfortable because you can maintain the illusion of competence while avoiding the reality of learning. Growth only happens when you're willing to be imperfect in motion rather than perfect in stillness.

Every time you avoid a challenge because you might not excel immediately, every time you spend hours polishing work that was already good enough, every time you stay silent in class because your answer might be wrong, you're not protecting your potential. You're shrinking it.

The people who are building expertise aren't the ones who never make mistakes. They're the ones making mistakes faster, learning from them, and moving forward. They start before they feel ready. They produce messy first drafts. They raise their hand when they're only seventy percent sure. They're willing to be bad at something before they're good at it, because they understand that's the only way it works.

There's an important distinction here though. This isn't about turning in careless work or abandoning your standards. Mistakes that come from lack of effort are avoidable and don't help you grow. Mistakes that come from attempting something genuinely difficult are unavoidable and essential.

When you're working at the edge of your ability, mistakes aren't a sign you're not good enough. They're a sign you're exactly where you need to be.

Chapter 8

Discipline Without Burnout

You've seen the social media posts celebrating all-nighters, heard people brag about how little sleep they got, watched classmates compete over who's more stressed. The culture around you treats exhaustion like a trophy, as if being tired proves you're serious about success.

The goal isn't just to survive high school or get into college. The goal of this time in your life is to build skills, confidence, and capacity that last beyond next semester. And you can't do that if you're running on empty, hating what you're doing, and counting down the days until you can finally stop.

Yes, you do need discipline. Growth requires consistent effort, and there's no way around that. What you need is sustainable effort – the kind of work that builds your skills instead of draining your capacity to think.

The difference between sustainable discipline and burnout culture comes down to this: burnout culture measures your worth by how much you suffer. Sustainable discipline measures your worth by how much you grow.

One leaves you exhausted and resentful. The other leaves you stronger and more capable.

You've probably felt the difference yourself. There are days when you work hard and feel energized, like you're building something real. And then there are days when you work hard and feel hollow, like you're just going through motions to avoid falling behind.

The first kind of work compounds over time, making you better. The second kind depletes you, leaving nothing in reserve when you need it.

Becoming someone who can work hard, think clearly, and keep growing without sacrificing your health, your relationships, or your sense of self; that's real discipline. And it's exactly what this chapter will help you build.

Sustainable Effort vs Burnout Culture: Why Exhaustion Isn't a Badge of Honor

You might see exhaustion as proof that you're working hard enough, as if being tired validates their commitment. But the World Health Organization doesn't classify burnout as a personal failure or a sign of weakness – it classifies it as an occupational phenomenon, a mismatch between what's being demanded and what's sustainable.

This distinction matters because it shifts the question from "Am I tough enough?" to "Is this actually working?"

The difference between sustainable effort and burnout culture comes down to what you're building versus what you're depleting. Sustainable effort strengthens your capacity over time. It leaves you more capable, more confident, more skilled than you were before.

Burnout culture does the opposite – it drains your reserves, weakens your focus, and leaves you running on fumes while pretending everything's fine.

Burnout culture is:

- Staying up until two in the morning to finish an assignment not because you're genuinely engaged but because you've been putting it off out of exhaustion.

- Bragging about how little sleep you got, as if surviving on four hours makes you more dedicated than someone who got seven.

- Feeling guilty for taking a break, even when your brain is too fried to absorb anything useful.

- Measuring your worth by how much you suffer rather than how much you grow.

The trap is that burnout culture often produces short-term results. You pull the all-nighter and turn in the paper. You cram for the test and pass. You push through exhaustion and maintain your GPA. For a while, it works – until it doesn't.

The problem is that this has no sustainability built in. There's no buffer for when you get sick, when life gets complicated, or when you simply need rest. And when you inevitably hit a wall, the culture tells you it's your fault for not being strong enough.

Research identifies six environmental factors that contribute to burnout, and none of them are about individual weakness:

- work overload
- lack of control
- insufficient rewards
- breakdown of community
- absence of fairness
- value conflicts

In school, that can look like too much on your plate with not enough support, expectations that don't account for how you actually learn, effort that nobody seems to notice, feeling isolated from the people around you, grading that feels inconsistent, or pressure to pursue a path that doesn't feel like yours.

Sustainable effort operates differently. It starts with a simple but powerful question: What's the amount of work you could do regularly without feeling desperate for the weekend?

If you can't take a day off when you're sick without everything collapsing, you're operating beyond sustainable capacity. If the thought of continuing at your current pace for another month fills you with dread, something needs to change, because the system isn't working.

Building sustainable effort means creating buffer time in your schedule, not operating at maximum capacity every single day. It means treating rest as productive, not as something you have to earn or feel guilty about. It means recognizing that small, consistent actions compound into significant growth, while intense bursts of unsustainable effort lead to burnout and backsliding.

People who succeed long-term aren't the ones who can endure the most suffering. They're the ones who learn to work hard in ways that build capacity over time. Real discipline means growing effectively without losing yourself in the process.

Smart Study Strategies: Working With Your Brain, Not Against It

Your brain isn't designed to absorb information through sheer force of will. It has specific patterns for how it learns best, and when you ignore those patterns, you end up working twice as hard for half the results.

The difference between struggling productively and just spinning your wheels comes down to whether you're using strategies that align with how your unique brain processes and retains information.

Strategy #1 – Retrieval Practice

One of the most powerful principles in learning science is retrieval practice – the act of pulling information from memory rather than passively reviewing it. When you force your brain to retrieve information, you strengthen the neural pathways that make that information accessible later.

This is why practice problems work better than reviewing formulas, and why explaining concepts out loud strengthens understanding more than silently reviewing definitions.

The mistake most students make is confusing familiarity with mastery. You read through your notes, recognize the information, and think "I know this." But recognition isn't the same as recall. When test day comes and you need to produce that information without prompts, the pathway isn't strong enough.

Retrieval practice builds that pathway by making your brain work to access the information repeatedly, even when it feels harder than just reviewing.

Strategy #2 – Spaced Repetition

Another strategy that works is spreading your study sessions out over time instead of cramming everything into one long session. Your brain consolidates information during the rest periods in between, which means studying for an hour on three separate days will stick better than grinding through three hours in one sitting.

Cramming might get you through tomorrow's test, but it doesn't build lasting understanding. The information goes into short-term memory and disappears within days because your brain never had the chance to move it into long-term storage. Spaced repetition works because each time you return to material after a gap, your brain has to work slightly harder to retrieve it, which strengthens the memory and makes it more durable.

Strategy #3 – Interleaving

Mixing different types of problems or subjects within a single study session also helps you learn more, even though it feels less comfortable than just doing the same type of problem over and over. When you only practice one kind of problem at a time, you're not really learning the material. You're just repeating a pattern.

Interleaving forces your brain to actively choose the right way to solve each problem, which builds the kind of flexible thinking that transfers to new situations.

These strategies share a common thread: they all involve making your brain work harder during practice so that performance becomes easier later. This is the opposite of what most students do when they choose study methods that feel easy and comfortable in the moment, then wonder why they struggle when it counts.

Strategy #4 – The Pomodoro Technique

Working with your brain also means respecting its need for breaks and recovery. The Pomodoro Technique – studying in focused intervals (typically twenty-five minutes) followed by short breaks – leverages the brain's natural attention span rather than fighting it.

The goal isn't to study longer. It's to study in ways that stick. When you use retrieval practice, space your sessions over time, interleave different types of problems, and build in strategic breaks, you're not just working hard – you're working smart. You're building understanding that lasts beyond the test, developing skills that compound over time, and protecting your capacity to think clearly instead of burning it out through ineffective grinding.

Building Habits That Compound: Small Consistent Actions That Create Exponential Growth

When it comes to building habits, consistency beats intensity every time. One study found that it takes an average of 66 days for a new behavior to become automatic, and anywhere from 18 to 254 days depending on how complex the habit is and how you're wired. The factor that mattered most wasn't how dramatically people changed. It was whether they kept showing up, even when it didn't feel like anything was happening.

This is where a lot of high achievers go wrong. The gap between putting in the work and actually seeing results creates a window where most people quit, convinced it isn't working. But that's exactly when it is working. Progress compounds quietly at first and then pays off in a big way later.

The key is choosing habits that build capacity rather than just checking boxes, because not all consistent actions compound equally. Recopying notes every day is consistent, but it doesn't strengthen understanding the way retrieval practice does. Highlighting textbooks is a habit, but it doesn't build thinking skills the way explaining concepts out loud does.

The habits that compound are the ones that make your brain work – retrieving information, solving problems, making connections, creating explanations.

Building habits that compound requires a kind of patience that feels totally unnatural when everything around you is designed for instant results. But if you can keep showing up with small, consistent actions even when nothing seems to be happening, the math works in your favor. The growth doesn't just add up. It multiplies. Six months from now you'll look back and barely recognize how much stronger you've become.

The difference between discipline that builds you and discipline that breaks you comes down to one question: Can you sustain this? Not just for this week or this semester, but for the long stretch of time it takes to develop real competence.

If the answer is no – if your current process requires you to sacrifice sleep, health, and any sense of balance just to keep up – then you're not building discipline. You're building a system designed to collapse.

Destroying your health, your relationships, and your ability to think clearly just to chase short-term results isn't strength. It's self-sabotage with a good work ethic on top. Real discipline means building something that lasts beyond this semester, this year, this phase of your life. It means becoming someone who can work hard, think clearly, and keep growing without losing yourself along the way.

You don't need to prove your worth through exhaustion. You need to protect your ability to think, learn, and grow – because that's what determines how far you'll go.

Chapter 9

Building Real Confidence

Real confidence doesn't come from telling yourself you're amazing. It doesn't come from a good grade on a test you crammed for, or from your parents saying you're smart, or from a motivational quote you saw on Instagram.

Those things might make you feel good temporarily, but that feeling evaporates the second you hit a real challenge or get feedback that stings.

Genuine confidence is built differently. It's constructed piece by piece, through accumulated evidence that you can handle hard things. It's the quiet certainty that comes from knowing you've struggled before and made it through. It's trusting yourself because you've given yourself reasons to.

This matters more now than ever because you're growing up in a world that offers constant shortcuts around the hard work that builds real capability. And deep down, you know when you've earned something versus when you've just performed well. That gap between how things look and what you know to be true is what creates the insecurity that no amount of positive self-talk can fix.

The difference between fake confidence and real confidence is evidence. Fake confidence needs constant reinforcement from external sources – compliments, grades, social media validation. Real confidence is self-sustaining because it's built on a foundation of documented capability.

When you know what you've overcome, when you can point to specific skills you've developed, when you have proof that you follow through on commitments to yourself, you don't need anyone else to convince you that you're capable.

When you build confidence you can take bigger risks, face harder challenges, and pursue opportunities that currently feel out of reach. You're building it so that when your brain whispers "you can't do this," you have a ready answer: "Actually, here's the evidence that I can."

Small Wins: Why Confidence Is Built One Piece of Evidence at a Time

Think about learning to ride a bike. Nobody gets on for the first time and immediately cruises down the street with perfect balance. You wobble for three feet before putting your foot down. Then five feet. Then ten.

Each tiny extension of balance is a small win, a piece of evidence that your body is learning something new. Eventually, those pieces stack up until you're riding without thinking about it, and your confidence isn't based on someone telling you that you can do it – it's because you already did.

This is how real confidence develops in every area. It's constructed through the accumulation of small, specific pieces of evidence that prove to your brain you're capable of more than you were yesterday.

The problem is that you're trained to focus only on big outcomes – the final grade, the championship game, the college acceptance. These high-stakes results feel like the only evidence that matters, which means every setback or mediocre performance feels like proof that you're not capable.

This creates a fragile form of confidence that collapses under pressure because it's built on outcomes you can't always control rather than on the process of getting better that you can.

Small wins shift the focus to what you can control: your effort, your strategies, your willingness to try again. When you start tracking evidence at this level, confidence becomes much more stable because it's not dependent on external validation or perfect results.

Small wins look like:

- Finally understanding a math concept you've been confused about for a week, even if you still get some practice problems wrong.
- Speaking up once in class when you usually stay silent.
- Rewriting a paragraph in your essay because you know it could be clearer, not because a teacher told you to.
- Studying for thirty focused minutes without checking your phone.
- Asking for help when you're stuck instead of pretending you understand.

None of these feel impressive in the moment. They don't come with applause or recognition. But each one is a data point that proves you're someone who shows up, who tries, who doesn't quit when things get uncomfortable.

Over time, these data points accumulate into a pattern, and that pattern becomes your identity.

The key is making these wins visible. Your brain needs to register that progress is happening, which means you can't just let small successes pass by unnoticed. This is where tracking becomes essential – not in an obsessive way, but in a way that creates a record you can look back on when doubt creeps in.

Athletes do this naturally by logging workouts and noting improvements in speed, endurance, or technique. You can do the same by keeping a simple list of concepts mastered, problems solved independently, or moments when they chose understanding over just getting the answer.

The format doesn't matter. What matters is creating concrete evidence that you're building capability, one piece at a time.

When you have this evidence, confidence stops being something you have to manufacture through positive self-talk. It becomes something you simply possess because you've proven to yourself, repeatedly, that you can handle hard things and come out stronger.

Skill Stacking: How Unrelated Abilities Compound Into Unique Competence

It's easy to think that you need to be exceptional at one thing to stand out. But there's a different thing that's often more powerful and more realistic: combining multiple decent skills into a unique combination that nobody else has.

This is called skill stacking, and it works because value doesn't just come from being the absolute best at something. Value comes from being able to do things that other people can't, and sometimes the most valuable capabilities emerge when you connect abilities that don't obviously belong together.

It's like a student who's decent at writing, reasonably good at research, and has developed some basic coding skills. None of these abilities alone makes them exceptional – there are better writers, stronger researchers, and far more advanced programmers in their school.

But the combination creates something unusual: they can build websites that clearly communicate complex information backed by solid evidence. That specific combination is rare, and it opens opportunities that mastering just one of those skills wouldn't provide.

These skills don't just sit separately in your brain waiting to be used one at a time. When you develop them intentionally and use them together repeatedly, they start to reinforce each other.

Better research improves your writing because you have stronger material to work with. Better writing improves how you present your code. Better coding gives you new ways to organize and display research. Each skill makes the others more effective.

This compounding effect is what makes skill stacking different from just picking up random things. The skills have to interact, which means you need to actually use them together in real situations, not just study them separately. An athlete who combines physical training with knowing how nutrition works and understanding the mental side of competition isn't just collecting knowledge. They're building something where each piece makes the others work better.

The process works in three predictable phases.

- Skill acquisition, where you're learning the basics and progress feels relatively quick.
- Skill integration, where you start trying to use multiple abilities together and everything feels harder because you're forcing your brain to coordinate different types of thinking. This middle phase is uncomfortable, and it's where most people quit because they mistake the difficulty for failure.
- Skill leverage, where the integration stabilizes and you start experiencing the compounding returns – your output increases without proportional effort because your skills are amplifying each other.

When building confidence, you're not trying to be the best at any single thing, which means you're not constantly comparing yourself to the top performer in each category. Instead, you're building a combination that's distinctively yours, which creates a different kind of confidence – the knowledge that you bring something to the table that others don't.

The confidence that emerges from skill stacking is durable because it's based on demonstrated capability to solve problems in ways that require your specific combination of abilities. You have proof that you can do things others can't, simply because you've built a stack they don't have.

Becoming Someone You Trust: Why Following Through on Small Promises Creates Unshakeable Confidence

When you say you'll do something and then actually do it – even when it's small, even when no one's watching – you're building evidence that you're someone who follows through. That evidence becomes the foundation of unshakeable confidence.

You may not realize how much damage broken self-promises cause, like when you tell yourself you'll start that project tonight, then you don't. You commit to studying for thirty minutes without your phone, then you check it after five. You promise yourself you'll ask that question in class tomorrow, then you stay silent.

Each broken promise might seem insignificant in the moment, but your brain is keeping score. Over time, these small betrayals teach you that you can't trust yourself, and that lack of self-trust is what makes confidence collapse under pressure.

Research on self-efficacy – your belief that you can do what you set out to do – shows that this kind of confidence gets earned through demonstrated competence, not positive thinking. You build it by doing things, not by telling yourself you can.

When you consistently follow through on commitments, your brain releases dopamine, reinforcing the neural pathways tied to reliability. That biological loop makes confidence self-perpetuating: each kept promise makes the next one a little easier to keep.

The key is starting with promises so small they feel almost trivial. You're committing to one specific action: finish this problem set before dinner, write for fifteen minutes, review notes for ten minutes before bed, speak up once in tomorrow's discussion. The size of the promise matters less than the act of keeping it.

This is fundamentally different from the hollow confidence that comes from hype or affirmations. That kind of confidence evaporates the moment you face real difficulty because it's not backed by evidence.

But confidence built on a track record of follow-through is resilient. When you hit a setback or struggle with something hard, you can think: "This specific task is challenging, but I have extensive evidence that I'm someone who persists and follows through. I've proven it to myself again and again."

The practice works best when you make your commitments visible. Keep a simple record, like a list on your phone, a notebook, a document, where you write down what you committed to and mark when you complete it.

Create concrete evidence you can reference when doubt creeps in. When your brain whispers that you're not capable or that you can't trust yourself to handle something difficult, you have proof to the contrary: a record of promises kept, challenges faced, commitments honored.

This works because it makes progress visible and achievable. Instead of waiting for dramatic breakthroughs or perfect performances, you're collecting evidence daily through manageable actions: understanding a concept you were confused about yesterday, speaking up when you usually stay quiet, choosing to struggle through a problem instead of immediately looking up the answer.

The foundation beneath all of this is self-trust, which is earned through keeping promises to yourself. This creates a form of confidence that's unshakeable because it's based on the simple fact that you've demonstrated, repeatedly, that you're someone who does what you say you'll do.

Real confidence isn't the absence of doubt or fear. It's having enough evidence of your own capability that doubt doesn't stop you from trying. It's knowing that even if this specific challenge is hard, you have a track record of facing hard things and coming out stronger. It's trusting yourself not because someone told you that you should, but because you've given yourself dozens of reasons to.

This is the confidence that lasts beyond high school, beyond the next test, beyond the moments when everything feels uncertain. It's built one small win at a time, one skill combination at a time, one kept promise at a time, until you're not someone trying to feel confident. You simply are confident, because the evidence is undeniable.

Conclusion

Everything you've read here only matters if you actually use it, and that starts with a single honest question:

What are you going to do differently tomorrow?

The difference between being smart and getting smart is about what you choose when things get hard. It's about whether you lean into struggle or run from it. It's about whether you're building real competence or just maintaining the appearance of success. Every time you face a difficult problem, every time you're tempted to take the shortcut, every time you feel that familiar fear of looking stupid, you're making a choice about who you're becoming.

You've learned that struggle isn't a sign you're not good enough. It's the feeling of your brain building new capacity. You've learned that AI can be a powerful tool or a dangerous crutch, depending entirely on how intentionally you use it. You've learned that perfectionism masquerades as high standards but actually keeps you stuck, afraid to attempt anything where you might fail. You've learned that the confidence you're seeking doesn't come from affirmations or good grades. It comes from accumulated evidence that you can handle hard things.

But knowing these things and living them are completely different. The real test isn't whether you understood the concepts in this book. It's whether you'll choose growth when it's uncomfortable, when nobody's watching, when the shortcut is right there and would be so much easier.

It's staying with the math problem for ten more minutes even though your brain is screaming to give up. It's asking the clarifying question in class even though you're afraid it sounds basic. It's using AI to check your thinking instead of replacing it. It's tracking your progress against your own past performance instead of comparing yourself to everyone else's highlight reel. It's choosing messy forward motion over perfect stagnation. It's building habits that compound instead of grinding until you burn out.

The world you're growing up in makes it easier than ever to look capable without becoming capable. You can generate essays, solve problems, and produce work that appears impressive while building almost nothing real underneath. That's the trap, and it's more dangerous than any previous generation has faced because the shortcuts are so seamless, so available, so tempting.

But real skill wins. Not eventually. Not in some distant future. Right now. The person who can actually think, who has built genuine competence through struggle, who has protected their ability to learn and adapt – that person has something no tool can replicate and no shortcut can fake.

Three years from now, five years from now, ten years from now, you'll be living with the choices you're making today. The thinking habits you're building right now will either serve you or limit you. The relationship you're developing with discomfort will either expand your capabilities or keep you trapped in an ever-shrinking comfort zone.

Your grades do matter. Colleges look at transcripts, scholarships depend on GPA, and yes, that chemistry test is real. But the thinking skills you build now, the resilience that comes from actual struggle, the confidence that comes from solving hard things yourself – those are what determine whether you can handle college, adapt when a job changes on you, navigate problems that don't come with answer keys.

Shortcuts work in the short term. You can use AI to write your essays, copy solutions to keep your grade up, optimize for performance without building real understanding. You might graduate with impressive stats.

But there's a difference between having credentials and having capacity. One of those you can fake. The other one you can't.

You don't need to be perfect. You don't need to transform overnight. You just need to choose growth one decision at a time, consistently, even when it's hard.

Especially when it's hard.

That's where real confidence comes from. That's where real capability is built. That's where you become someone you can trust.

The work starts now.

Thank You for Reading!

I hope you found *Beyond Good Grades*

helpful and enjoyable!

Your feedback is invaluable to me and helps others
discover this book.

If you could take a moment to leave a review, I'd greatly
appreciate it. Scan the QR code below to leave your review:

Thank you!

Patty

Visit the Cantelune Press website for more compassionate
books that meet you where you are!
https://cantelunepress.com/

Bibliography

Keluskar, J.L. (2026, February 16). *Dealing With The Fear Of Looking Dumb*. The Minds Journal.

Brain Botanics. (n.d.). *Conquering the Fear of Looking Stupid: Tips to Boost Your Confidence*. Brain Botanics.

National Center for Biotechnology Information. (n.d.). *Checking your browser before accessing pmc.ncbi.nlm.nih.gov*. PubMed Central.

Dr. Jen. (2018, May 30). *Why Do Teens Do Stupid Things?* Dr. Jen.

Pickhardt, C.E. (2022, March 14). *Adolescence and the Age of Painful Embarrassment*. Psychology Today.

Lara, M. (2024, September 16). *Life Skills For Teens Toolkit: Master A Growth Mindset, Emotions, Financial Savviness, Cybersmarts & More, Even Though It Seems Like Everyone Else Has It Figured Out*. Goodreads.

Sheppard, S. (n.d.). *A Growth Mindset for Teens*. Barnes & Noble.

Underwood, A. (2025, March 13). *The Silent Struggle: Teen and Young Adult Self-Esteem, Fear, and Identity*. Amy Underwood Therapy.

Lightfully Behavioral Health. (n.d.). *21 Ways You Can Help Your Teen Combat the Feeling of Failure*. Lightfully Behavioral Health.

Weill Cornell Medical College. (2012, September 27). *Learning to Overcome Fear is Difficult for Teens*. Weill Cornell Medicine Newsroom.

Chicago Counseling and Therapy. (n.d.). *Overcoming Fear of Failure: Helping Teens Reframe Mistakes*. Chicago Counseling and Therapy.

Child Therapy Center LA. (n.d.). *Understanding and Addressing Low Self-Esteem in Teens*. Child Therapy Center LA.

American Academy of Child and Adolescent Psychiatry. (2017, September). *Teen Brain: Behavior, Problem Solving, and Decision Making*. American Academy of Child and Adolescent Psychiatry.

Deepsky Leaders. (n.d.). *The Silent Conversation: Understanding Your Inner Voice*. Deepsky Leaders.

Smith, J. (2025, October 28). *Growth Mindset vs Fixed Mindset: How what you think affects what you achieve*. Nerva Health.

ActivStars. (2025, May 30). *Growth Mindset in Sports: How to Learn from Mistakes and Keep Improving*. ActivStars Blog.

Tiny Tekkers. (2024, September 4). *Encouraging a Growth Mindset in Young Athletes*. Tiny Tekkers.

i9 Sports. (2021, July 30). *The Role of Friendships in Youth Sports*. i9 Sports.

Coaching the Coaches. (2019, July 15). *Growth Mindset: Gimmik or Growing Impact*. Coaching the Coaches.

Feith, J. (2022, March 3). *How To Support A Growth Mindset In Physical Education*. The Physical Educator.

Discover Saha. (n.d.). *The Fixed Mindset Trap: Why Positive Labeling Can Be Detrimental to a Child's Development*. Discover Saha.

Chambliss, C. (2019, September 12). *Fixed Versus Growth Mindset in Childhood and Subsequent Depression Risk*. Journal of Psychiatry Depression & Anxiety.

Cote, C. (2022, March 10). *Growth Mindset vs. Fixed Mindset: What's the Difference?*. Harvard Business School Online Business Insights Blog.

Hinds, B. F. (n.d.). *Putting Growth Mindset into Action: Labels Without Limits*. AMISA.

Hull, B.. (n.d.). *The Benefits of a Growth Mindset & Dangers of a Fixed Mindset*. Cengage Blog.

Blad, E. (2025, April 14). *What Are Grades Really For? What Research Says About 4 Common Answers*. Education Week.

Madeleine. (2021, March 26). *Grades vs Educational Knowledge*. Chapman Learning Commons.

National Center for Biotechnology Information. (n.d.). *Checking your browser before accessing pmc.ncbi.nlm.nih.gov*. PubMed Central.

Marco Learning. (n.d.). *Grades vs Learning – Shifting Attention to What's Important*. Marco Learning.

Arundel, K. (2024, August 5). *Nearly 60% of grades don't match student test scores*. K-12 Dive.

Puutio, T. A. (2025, August 4). *Born Smart or Built Smart? The Truth About Intelligence and Effort*. Psychology Today.

Menier, N. (2025, September 11). *This is what science says about being born smart vs becoming smart*. Le Ravi.

Askew, K. (2025, September 16). *The Hidden Cost of Academic Perfectionism*. Lightspeed Systems.

National Center for Biotechnology Information. (n.d.). *Past studies suggest that the adaptive or maladaptive consequences of inflated self-estimate, one form of positive illusions, require further investigation*. PubMed.

Sohn, E. (2024, October 1). *Perfectionism and the high-stakes culture of success: The hidden toll on kids and parents*. Monitor on Psychology.

Schiller International University. (n.d.). *The Impact of Artificial Intelligence on Higher Education: How It Is Transforming Learning*. Schiller International University.

Office of Communications, College of Education. (2024, October 24). *AI in Schools: Pros and Cons*. College of Education.

National Center for Biotechnology Information. (n.d.). *Checking your browser before accessing pmc.ncbi.nlm.nih.gov*. PubMed Central.

Healey, M. (2025, December 9). *The Pros and Cons of AI in Education: Benefits, Risks, and Real Examples*. Discovery Education.

George Lucas Educational Foundation. (n.d.). *How AI Vaporizes Long-Term Learning*. Edutopia.

Growth Wise. (2020, September 24). *With Tests, Take a Growth Mindset*. Growth Wise.

Fletcher-Wood, H. (2022, March 6). *Is growth mindset real? New evidence, new conclusions*. Improving Teaching.

Loper, C. (2021, May 16). *Growth mindsets debunked? Not so fast*. NW Tutoring.

Kaufman, S.B. (2023, December 28). *Growth Mindset Theory: What's the Actual Evidence?*. Beautiful Minds Newsletter.

Psychology Today. (n.d.). *Growth Mindset Test*. Psychology Today.

Morehead, J. (2012, June 19). *Stanford University's Carol Dweck on the Growth Mindset and Education*. OneDublin.org.

TherapyDen. (n.d.). *Growth Mindset Test: Where Do You Fall, Fixed or Growth?*. TherapyDen.

Ross, D. (2026, January 8). *Can AI Tutors Promote a True Growth Mindset? Exploring the Risks and Promise of Custom GPTs in Education*. Getting Smart.

Gaehde, N. (2025, November 21). *Using Technology to Power a Growth Mindset in the Classroom*. Cambium Learning Group.

Clark, L. (n.d.). *Unlocking AI's Potential: Why a Growth Mindset is Key*. GP Strategies.

Nezich, H. (2024, October 15). *Nurturing a Growth Mindset in the AI Era*. ASE.

Murphy, Y.G. (n.d.). *AI and the Future of Human-Guided Learning: An Artificial Intelligence (AI) Roundup*. CE International.

Shaikley, L. (2025, September 4). *Your comfort zone is shrinking (and it's kinda your fault)*. Things you'll learn the hard way (but wish you didn't).

The Psych Collective. (n.d.). *Comfort*. The Psych Collective.

O'Brien, N. (n.d.). *Growth happens when you operate on the edge of your comfort zone*. A Lust for Life.

American Psychiatric Association. (2022, August 05). *Can Mindset Training Reduce Student Stress?*. American Psychiatric Association.

QEP Committee. (2023, March 21). *Adopt a Growth Mindset for a Better Life*. Daily Dose TTUHSC.

National Center for Biotechnology Information. (n.d.). *PMC12109404*. PubMed Central.

National Center for Biotechnology Information. (n.d.). *PMC9046553*. PubMed Central.

Le Cunff, A..(n.d.). *From fixed mindset to growth mindset: the complete guide*. Ness Labs.

Huberman, A.D. (n.d.). *Dr. David Yeager: How to Master Growth Mindset to Improve Performance*. Huberman Lab.

Schiavone, A. (2020, July 23). *The Comparison Trap - How Social Media is Ruining Your Mental Health*. Mind Muscle.

Murphy, J. (2022, September 15). *How to Break Out of the Social Media Comparison Trap*. Wondermind.

Olele, I. (n.d.). *The Social Media Comparison Trap*. Genesis Psychiatric Solutions.

Fort, D. (2023, March 28). *How to Get Out of the Social Media Comparison Trap*. CCCRD.

JED Foundation. (n.d.). *Understanding Social Comparison on Social Media*. JED Foundation.

Tubb, R. (n.d.). *Social Networking is a Life's Highlight Reel, Not the Whole Story*. Tubblog.

Verily. (2019, July 8). *Yes, Social Media Is a Highlight Reel – And That's Okay*. Verily.

Tava Health. (December 16, 2024). *Guide to Developing a Growth Mindset*. Tava Health.

Purdue Global. (2024, January 8). *What Is a Growth Mindset and How Can You Develop One?*. Purdue Global.

Palmer, M. (2025, October 2). *What is a Growth Mindset?*. Southern New Hampshire University.

Western Governors University. (2019, April 12). *What Is A Growth Mindset? 8 Steps To Develop One*. WGU.

Emanuele, G. (2020, March 2). *How to Build a Growth Mindset*. Galen Emanuele | Team Culture & Leadership Keynotes.

House, P. (2022, December 22). *You Are Your Mindset A Growth Mindset for Teens: Practical Lessons & Activities to Build Confidence, Problem Solve, Grow Skills, and Become R, (Paperback)*. Walmart.

Sheppard, S. (2022, December 22). *A Growth Mindset for Teens: Practical Lessons & Activities to Build Confidence, Problem Solve, Grow Skills, and Become Resilient in 31days..* Magers & Quinn Booksellers.

Sheppard, S. (2022, November 21). *A Growth Mindset For Teens: Practical Lessons & Activities To Build Confidence, Problem Solve, Grow Skills, And Become Resilient in 31 Days.* Goodreads.

Prasid. (2024, October 18). *Embrace the Mess: Why Perfection is the Enemy of Progress.* The Growth CMO with Prasid.

Clark, K. (2024, February 14). *Choose Progress Over Perfection: Embrace Messy Action.* Your Insight Coach.

Patterson, M. (2025, December 1). *The Delight of Progress (Not Perfection).* BS-Free Business.

Tessa. (May 22, 2025). *Choose Progress over Perfection to Level Up Your Life.* Tessa Hill.

Miker, S. (2025, April 22). *Progress Over Perfection: How to Stop Holding Yourself Back.* Scott Miker.

Stinson, T. (2025, July 07). *Progress Over Perfection: 10 Steps to Start Before You're Ready.* Tina Stinson Wellness.

Curtis, M. (2024, September 29). *The Burnout Trap of Hustle Culture and Why Sustainable Change Matters.* Martha Curtis Coaching.

Stanley, A.J. (2026, February 2). *Learning Design Beyond Burnout: Building Sustainable Practices with AI.* Learning Guild.

Loy, J. (2022, April 14). *Beat burnout and overcome grind culture by becoming more sustainably-minded.* Miami University.

Demsky, C. (2023, February 6). *Faculty Burnout & Sustainability.* Oakland University Center for Excellence in Teaching and Learning.

Pierce, R. (2023, September 26). *15 Strategies for Cultivating a Growth Mindset for Teens.* Life Skills Advocate.

Schwarz, N. (n.d.). *How to Teach Growth Mindset to Teens.* Big Life Journal.

The Second Step® Team. (2024, September 18). *Growth Mindset Strategies to Shift Student Perspectives.* Second Step.

Barry, K. (n.d.). *Enhancing Growth Mindset.* Teaching Inclusively | Teaching Strategies.

Thompson, S. (2025, December 11). *Why A Growth Mindset Beats Natural Talent for Building New Habits.* Ahead.

Routinery. (2024, February 16). *The Power of Compound Habits: Small Changes, Big Results.* Routine & Habit Tracker App Tips.

Ava Mind. (n.d.). *Building Confidence Through Small Wins: A Practical Guide.* Ava Mind.

Magnet ABA. (n.d.). *Understanding the Significance of Small Wins in Therapy and Recovery*. Magnet ABA.

Marley, N. (2025, January 23). *The Power of Small Wins: Using Process Goals to Build Momentum and Self-Belief*. The Mental Game.

Thomas, K. (2025, September 12). *The Power of Small Wins – Building Confidence One Workout at a Time*. Sport Speed Lab.

Matovu K. K. (2026, January 1). *How Skill Stacking Actually Works Over Time*. Blinkerhub.

Ames, E. (2023, August 23). *The Art of Skill Stacking: Maximizing Your Skills Portfolio*. tilr.

Real Social Skills. (n.d.). *Real Social Skills*. Real Social Skills. [

Whole Child Counseling. (n.d.). *18 growth mindset books for kids about mistakes, art, and the power of yet*. Whole Child Counseling.

Microcosm Coaching. (2020, April 12). *How To Cultivate A Long-Term Growth Mindset in Training*. Microcosm Coaching.

Brodersen, M.. (2020, November 01). *The Growing Importance of College and Career Readiness Indicators*. Institute of Education Sciences.

National College and Career Readiness Indicators. (n.d.). *College Ready*. Redefining Ready.

Alliance for Excellent Education. (2023, February). *Undermeasuring: College and Career Readiness Indicators May Not Reflect College and Career Outcomes*. Alliance for Excellent Education.